Boat Diving

SS/®

SCUBA SCHOOLS
INTERNATIONAL

DISCLAIMER:

The information contained in the SSI training materials is intended to give an individual enrolled in a training course a broad perspective of the diving activity. There are many recommendations and suggestions regarding the use of standard and specialized equipment for the activity. Not all of the equipment discussed in the training material can, or will, be used in this activity. The choice of equipment and techniques used in the course is determined by the location of the activity, the environmental conditions and other factors.

A choice of equipment and techniques cannot be made until the dive site is surveyed immediately prior to the dive. Based on the dive site, the decision should be made regarding which equipment and techniques shall be used. The decision belongs to the dive leader and the individual enrolled in the training course.

The intent of all SSI training materials is to give individuals as much information as possible in order for individuals to make their own decisions regarding the diving activity, what equipment should be used and what specific techniques may be needed. The ultimate decision on when and how to dive is for the individual diver to make.

First Edition
   First Printing, 12/90
       Revised, 4/96
       Revised, 6/98
   Second Printing, 07/00

Second Edition
   First Printing, 03/04

PRINTED IN THE USA

SCUBA SCHOOLS
INTERNATIONAL

2619 Canton Court • Fort Collins, CO 80525-4498
(970) 482-0883 • Fax (970) 482-6157

Contents

Section 4: Diving from Your Boat

Section 5: Finishing Your Boat Trip

Appendix

Acknowledgements

Editor in Chief	Gary Clark
Writers	James E. Bruning Gary Clark
Manager of Development	James E. Bruning
Graphic Designers	Jennifer Silos, Lori Evans, David Pratt
Cover Photo	Randy Pfizenmaier
Photographers	James E. Bruning, Randy Pfizenmaier
Contributing Photographers	Black Durgeon, Paolo Lilla, Rick Murchison
Technical Editors	Walt Amidon, Dan Barrows, Daryl Bauer, James Bruning, Ed Christini, Robert Kennedy, Doug McNeese, Kirk Mortensen, Linda Nelson, Eric Peterson, Jeff Powelson, Dennis Pulley, Warren Roseberry, Ed Salamone, Craig Simons, Sid Stovall, Ron Tinker, Craig Willemsen, Marjorie Young

Special thanks to the staff at Ocean Sports, Randy Pfizenmaier and Ikelite for going the extra mile in the production of this manual.

Preface

You will see that each section includes several unique icons to highlight information or add information that relates to the text near it. In some cases, these icons point out information directly associated with the section objectives, while in other cases, the icon indicates a continuing education opportunity. While these icons are designed to help you learn and retain information, they also provide you with an easy reference to important information as you study.

Pearl

"Pearl" the oyster (originally named "Hey!"), is found throughout the text to point out information that we believe is key to a new diver's success. The "pearls of wisdom" that our oyster friend highlights are designed to help you meet section objectives, assist in answering study guide questions and may be used in group discussions with your instructor.

Continuing Education

At Scuba Schools International, we believe that one of the keys to achieving and maintaining success as a diver is taking the "next step" via continuing education. To reinforce that belief, we have put a Continuing Education icon next to topics that correspond to continuing education opportunities available to you through your SSI Dealer. Your SSI Instructor or Dealer will be happy to answer any questions you may have about the continuing education courses listed throughout this manual.

Environment

SSI has always supported and promoted environmental awareness and believes that care for the environment should be a standard part of diver education from start to finish. For these reasons, an environmental icon has been included to highlight important environmental issues as they relate to divers and the underwater world. Topics that you will find the environmental icon next to include the importance of buoyancy control, reef appreciation and conservation, and using your equipment in an environmentally friendly way.

International Use

To meet international English language recommendations, some of the words you come across in this manual may look misspelled. The following is a list of these words in American English and their International counterparts.

American English	International Counterpart
Center	Centre
Meter	Metre
Gray	Grey
Aluminum	Aluminium

Throughout the manual, imperial measurements are listed first followed by the metric conversion. The following conversion units were used to convert the various measurements:

1 ATA (Atmospheres Absolute) = 14.7 psi (pounds per square inch)

1 ATA = 33 fsw (feet of sea water)

1 ATA = 10.33 metres of sea water

1 ATA = 1 bar

1 Metre = 3.28 feet

$C° = (F° -32) ÷ 1.8$

1 kg (kilogram) = 2.2 lbs (pounds)

1 km (kilometre) = .621 miles

Note: For greater ease, many of the conversions in this text have been rounded to the nearest whole number, and may not reflect the exact conversion.

Be Ready for Your Journey

Intro

Welcome

To be a diver that is completely prepared for any diving situation that may occur, you will need the experience and training gained from SSI Specialty Courses. Taking our courses is your chance to begin a journey that explores beyond the surface of diving. The great thing is that with each specialty course you take, you are simultaneously earning credit towards higher levels of diver ratings, such as Specialty Diver, Advanced Open Water Diver, Master Diver, Dive Control Specialist, and Open Water Instructor. It is up to you to decide how far you want to go.

Each course will provide you with the proper knowledge and skills to truly consider yourself an experienced diver. Our goal is to prepare you for the adventure that lies ahead, as well as make sure you have a good time doing it!

The Diver Diamond

Each of our specialty courses is based on our Diver Diamond methodology, which focuses on the proper knowledge, skills, equipment and experience required to help you become a proficient diver.

Proper Knowledge

By using the SSI Continuing Education Program you will acquire knowledge about specific types of specialty diving that would take you years of diving to learn on your own.

Proper Skills

Under the guidance of an SSI Instructor, you will learn the correct skills and techniques associated with the specialties of your choice to make you a more comfortable and confident diver.

Proper Equipment

You will learn how to use an expanded range of equipment to help you make your dives more enjoyable and worthwhile.

Proper Experience

Your SSI Instructor has a wealth of experience to share with you during your course.

How Far Do You Want to Go?

Taking a specific number of specialties and continuing your pursuit of dives allows you to earn higher levels of diver ratings.

SSI's ratings are the only ratings in the industry that combine training and experience requirements, proving that SSI ratings are truly earned.

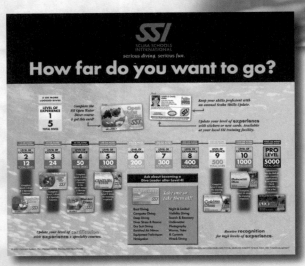

SSI Specialty Diver

SSI's intermediate diver rating is higher than any other agency's advanced courses. To earn the certification for Specialty Diver, you must complete 2 specialty courses and have done a total of 12 dives.

SSI Advanced
Open Water Diver

SSI's Advanced Diver rating stands alone in the industry with the highest combination of diving knowledge and experience. No other agency's advanced diver level compares. To earn the certification for Advanced Open Water Diver, you must complete 4 specialty courses and have done a total of 24 dives.

SSI Master Diver

SSI's Master Diver rating is one of the most elite ratings in diving today. Divers that have completed this level have combined the knowledge, skills and experience to truly call themselves Master Divers. To earn the certification for Master Diver, you must complete 5 specialty courses and have done a total of 50 dives.

SSI LEVEL 2 — 12 OR MORE LOGGED DIVES — LEVEL OF EXPERIENCE: 2 — 12 TOTAL DIVES

SSI LEVEL 3 — 24 OR MORE LOGGED DIVES — LEVEL OF EXPERIENCE: 3 — 24 TOTAL DIVES

SSI LEVEL 4 — 50 OR MORE LOGGED DIVES — LEVEL OF EXPERIENCE: 4 — 50 TOTAL DIVES

SSI Dive Control Specialist

This is SSI's initial dive leadership level. You receive both dive master and assistant instructor training, which means you can act not only as a Dive Master and lead groups of divers, but you can assist SSI Instructors in SSI courses. Dive Cons can also teach a select number of SSI Specialty Courses.

DIVE CONTROL SPECIALIST

Level 4 diver (60 Dives)
18 years old
Advanced Open Water Diver certified
Diver Stress & Rescue certified
Take Dive Control Specialist Course

SSI Open Water Instructor

The SSI Instructor Training Course (ITC) prepares you to become an active member of the scuba industry, a successful educator, and a valuable dive business employee.

OPEN WATER INSTRUCTOR

Level 5 diver (100 Dives)
18 years old
DiveCon certified
Take Instructor Training Course
Get instructor evaluation

Continuing Education is exciting and limitless. It is your chance to begin exploring below the surface. By utilizing SSI's various specialty courses you can acquire the knowledge and skills needed to be ready for some serious diving and serious fun!

Course Menu

- Boat Diving
- Computer Diving
- Deep Diving
- Diver Stress & Rescue
- Dry Suit Diving
- Enriched Air Nitrox
- Equipment Techniques
- Navigation
- Night & Limited Visibility Diving
- Search & Recovery
- Underwater Photography
- Waves, Tides & Currents
- Wreck Diving

Leadership Courses ▶

First Aid & CPR Training ▶

- Dive Control Specialist
- Open Water Instructor
- Scuba Rangers Instructor
- React Right Instructor

- React Right

Check with your SSI Dealer for availability and class schedules.

Intro

About SSI

Scuba Schools International is a worldwide diver certification agency and educational support organization. Recognized as an innovative leader in diver education, we create state-of-the-art training programs, training standards and materials for all levels of diver education.

The SSI Organization is set up to deliver quality. SSI Instructors can only teach at SSI Training Facilities, which are carefully screened to ensure they meet our standards. SSI Instructors use our highly-effective water training method called Comfort Through Repetition. Scuba skills become second nature, so you can relax and enjoy yourself when you go diving.

SSI is the only organization in the industry with this level of quality control and accountability. This means you can have confidence in everyone associated with Scuba Schools International.

SSI divers are respected all over the world because of SSI's reputation for training excellent divers. With over 1,900 Authorized Dealers in 90 countries, your SSI certification card will be welcomed anywhere you want to dive.

Mission

SSI's mission is to get people excited about diving as a lifetime of adventure. The key to a lifetime of diving is that people must have fun diving or they will choose to do something else. Our belief is that proper training has a lot to do with fun.

This is why we take training so seriously, because we take our fun so seriously. And that is why SSI Divers have such a long-standing reputation for being confident, competent, comfortable, outstanding divers — and they have the most fun too!

History

SSI was founded in 1970 and is the largest school-based training agency in the world.

In the Spring of 1999, SSI merged with the National Association of Scuba Diving Schools (NASDS founded in 1967) and created a new synergy in the dive industry. The sales and marketing expertise of NASDS, when joined with the renowned educational products of SSI, created a stronger company that is in a better position to serve dealers, instructors, and ultimately, divers.

Together, SSI and NASDS are responsible for a remarkable list of innovations and consequently have been recognized with the highest honors in the diving industry. Some of our most noteworthy accomplishments include:

First

◆ To require open water classes for certification.

◆ Integrated teaching systems.

◆ To require six open water dives for certification.

◆ To create a sales and marketing program to benefit retailers.

◆ To require visual inspections of cylinders.

◆ To introduce a buoyancy compensator device.

◆ To introduce an alternate second-stage.

◆ Full-motion video training system.

◆ Equipment inspection program.

◆ Risk awareness video.

◆ To develop a total dive log and recognition system.

And

◆ Bob Clark, founder of SSI, and John Gaffney, founder of NASDS, are both given the "Reaching Out Award" and inducted into the scuba industry's hall of fame in 1999.

Ed Christini received the "Reaching Out Award" and was inducted into the hall of fame in 2003.

◆ Also in 1999, Bob Clark is honored with the prestigious NOGI award for his contributions to dive education; an award also previously given to John Gaffney.

Intro

Worldwide

Since the first SSI Regional Centre opened in Southeast Asia in 1983, SSI has expanded around the world at a very rapid pace. This helps ensure that SSI Certification Cards are welcomed all over the planet, wherever you choose to dive.

Each regional centre is operated by a professional staff that handles everything from certification card production to training of SSI Instructors. And because the marketplace is often different from country to country, SSI Regional Centre have some latitude to adapt the SSI system to meet the needs of divers in their region.

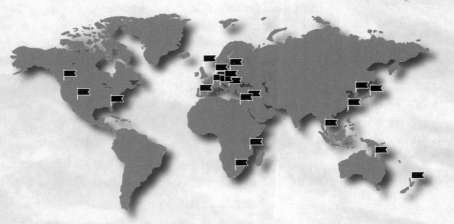

Involvement

As well as being a leader in the scuba industry, SSI was one of the founding members of the Recreational Scuba Training Council (RSTC), and was crucial in the development of the Universal Referral Program (URP).

We are certain that your journey through *Boat Diving* will be everything you imagined and more. Now, let's go have some fun!

Selecting Your Dive Boat

SECTION I

The first step in diving from boats is selecting one. Boats come in a wide variety of shapes, sizes, styles, and prices. Some cater to beginning divers, others to advanced divers. Most differ by the services they offer and the areas they dive. Selecting a boat is a matter of determining the type of diving you want to do and finding one that meets your needs.

Section 1 Objectives
After completing this section you will:

◆ Know the different types of boats available,

◆ Know how to select a boat charter that suits your needs,

◆ Know the boat's safety equipment and procedures.

Types of Boats

There are boats you live on, boats you spend the entire day on, and boats that shuttle you to the dive site and back.

Once you know what you need, you can judge the features of the boat and the type of trip it is taking.

An important factor is the boat's safety equipment and procedures. To reach your decision, weigh all the input and look for the best fit.

1

Types of Boats

There are three categories of boats we will cover in the Boat Diving Specialty manual: Live-aboards, Day boats, and Personal boats. Each has unique attributes making it ideal for a certain kind of diving. Which one you select will depend on how much diving you want to do, the kind of diving you want to do, and how much money you want to spend.

Luxury Live-Aboard Boat

Live-Aboards

These are large, comfortable boats designed to stay at sea for extended periods of time. Passengers live on board and dive from the boat. These boats feature showers, meals, beds, and an on-board air station. There are a wide variety of live-aboards, ranging from cruise liners designed for divers to smaller boats designed for weekend excursions. The cruise liners hold hundreds of divers and shuttle them to dive sites on smaller boats. They have all the comforts and conveniences that other cruise ships are famous for. The weekend live-aboards are smaller boats that are modest, but comfortable. There is also a fleet of luxury live-aboards harbored in the Caribbean and Pacific islands. The biggest benefit of live-aboards is the tremendous amount of diving you can do, and the increased accessibility to unspoiled dive spots, due to their increased range. Because your equipment is always ready to go, and because the boat is constantly stopping at great dive spots, it is easy for you to slip into the water. The only thing holding you back is your dive profile.

Live-Aboard Boat

Why Try a Live-Aboard?

Live-aboards are great for people who want to dive as much as possible.

DIVER DIAMOND
SSI
KNOWLEDGE • SKILLS • EQUIPMENT • EXPERIENCE

Day Boats

These boats take passengers to selected dive sites within a distance easily covered in one half day to one full day. In the U.S., Coast Guard licensing regulations split boats into two size categories: those carrying up to six passengers, called "six-packs," and those carrying more than six passengers. To carry fewer than six passengers the operator is required to be licensed by the U.S.C.G.. To carry more than six, both the operator and the boat need to be licensed. Sometimes, the larger day boats are live-aboards without overnight bookings, filling the slack time. In that case, they would have all the nice features such as showers and a galley. Smaller boats may include lunch or drinks. Typically, unless there is a compressor aboard, the number of dives is determined by the number of cylinders taken. The nice thing about day boats is their flexibility. You dive the days you want and, because of the number of operators, you have a variety of choices and options.

Day Boat

Day Boat/Live-Aboard Boat

Personal Boats

This category covers inflatable and other diving boats not for hire. Inflatable boats are quite popular because they are easy to handle, almost impossible to capsize, and can carry many people with equipment. Another functional design is the center console boat. These have plenty of deck room and storage, and handle well in rough water. Both inflatable and center console boats stay closer to shore on shorter day trips. For longer, overnight trips, the cuddy cabin boat is frequently used. It features a small forward cabin that usually contains a head and enough room to sleep two people. There are many designs available and safety should be your first consideration. To operate your personal boat properly, take a course in boat operation and handling.

Inflatable Rubber Boat

Determine Your Needs

One of the most important steps in selecting a dive boat is determining your needs. It is the only way you can accurately judge whether a boat is right for you. Also, by knowing what you want, you can focus on boats offering it, and not waste time and money on those that do not.

The Personal Boat

For any personal boat, the advantage is the ultimate freedom to explore and dive wherever the owner wants.

DIVER
DIAMOND
SSI
KNOWLEDGE · SKILLS · EQUIPMENT · EXPERIENCE

How Much Diving do You Plan to do?

Some people plan to dive every available minute. A live-aboard would give them all they could handle. Still others want to dive just a couple of times the whole vacation. They should look at day boats. Knowing how much diving you want to do will help you focus on the right boat for you.

What Type of Diving Do You Want to Do?

There are many kinds of diving, and they do not all mix together. Some boats cater to certain kinds of divers or feature certain kinds of dives, such as abalone hunts, wreck dives, night dives or wall dives. Photography or fish watching are compatible with almost anything. Live-aboards will include most styles, while day boats tend to have a plan in mind for each dive that day. Knowing what you want to accomplish will help you select the appropriate boat for you.

How Much Money do You Plan to Spend?

This applies more to day boats and live-aboards than personal boats. Day boats and live-aboards charge a wide range of prices and offer differing services for the price. To sort out the best value, consider what each boat offers. For example, some charge for air, nitrox and food, while others include that in the price.

Dive Boat Features

When sizing up a dive boat, regardless of the type, there are features to look for that make it more comfortable, functional, and safer for diving. Not all vessels will have all features listed below, so prioritize which ones are most important for your individual diving needs.

Length of the Boat

Larger boats usually ride better on rough water and hold more people, while smaller boats are usually faster and can anchor closer to dive sites.

Speed of the Boat

Especially for long trips, the speed of the boat makes a big difference in travel time.

Diver Capacity

In American waters, the Coast Guard regulates the capacity. This is not so outside the U.S., so determine if the boat looks like it will comfortably handle the maximum stated. The number of divers is both a safety and enjoyment factor. Large groups can present a chaotic situation, even on boats designed to accommodate them.

On-Board Compressor and Nitrox

Only larger boats have these, but they are nice for multiple dives. With a compressor you do not need multiple cylinders, you refill them.

On-Board Bathroom

For long stays on the water, they are an essential comfort.

Fresh Drinking Water (or Other Beverages)

To avoid dehydration on long, hot days, adequate beverages are essential. Breathing dry, compressed air will make you thirsty, as will salt water. Remember, nothing rehydrates better than drinking clean, fresh water.

On-Board Compressor

Safe Entry and Exit Points

Special ladders and platforms are best for getting into and out of the water.

Depth Sounding Equipment and GPS

These are useful for locating reefs and wrecks. Global Positioning Systems (GPS) are also handy for finding those hard to locate spots.

Sun and Wind Cover

It is wise to have some protection and shelter from excessive sun and wind exposure. Without it, you could have problems with sunburn and heat exhaustion, or cold.

Diving Platform

Game Holding Containers

If you take game, having a proper place to put it prevents spoilage and is considerate to others.

Salt Water Dunking Tank

Salt Water Mask Rinsing Tank

Some ocean boats have large containers filled with salt water used to rinse masks. Usually it is located near entry/exit points. On rough water it is safer than leaning over the platform and risking a premature plunge in the water.

Fresh Water Rinsing Tank

They are used mostly for washing off cameras after the dive. Cameras are sensitive to salt buildup and need frequent rinsing. Avoid dunking other equipment in this cylinder. Rinse masks in the salt water dunking cylinder.

Fresh Water Shower

After diving in salt water, it is good to rinse off your equipment and yourself with fresh water. Salt water damages equipment if it is not washed off.

Trip Considerations

Even if the boat looks right, you should also consider the diving it provides, how much it costs, and who is in charge. These factors can make or break a trip and, on same boat, can change from trip to trip. If there are several to choose from, select the boat most compatible with your diving style and ability.

Fresh Water Shower

Dive Plan

The captain and crew will select the site based on the needs of the majority. Make sure it is a dive you want to be a part of. For instance, if you want an advanced dive, do not go on a boat with students. On the other hand, if you have never dived in the ocean, do not go with a group looking for a challenging deep dive, especially if you have not been trained in specialty areas. Usually, sightseers and photographers blend well, but game collectors and entry level divers do not. Find out what type of dive is planned before you sign up.

Buddy Availability

If you do not have a diving partner, there is usually someone on the boat available to dive with you. However, these people can range from the boat's instructor or DiveCon to someone making their first dive after certification. When considering a dive buddy, you must ask yourself: are you comfortable with them? To make the decision, take their diving skill, your diving skill, and the water conditions into consideration. For instance, difficult drift dives should be done with an experienced diver. On the other hand, most shallow dives can be made fairly easily even with a beginning diver. If you are not comfortable with your assigned buddy, do not go on the dive.

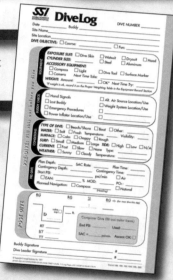

Use the SSI Total DiveLog check list to help you with your buddy check.

Captain and Crew

The captain and crew are as important as the boat. A good boat with a bad operator could spoil your trip. Bad operators not only ruin the fun, but they can be dangerous. Check the safety record and reputation of those in charge before signing up. Also, it is beneficial if the captain or crew speak your language and are certified at a diving leadership level.

Prices and Value

Compare prices and what you receive in return. Many boats include cylinders and weights, and some also include food, drinks or cylinder refills. Cleaner, nicer boats usually cost more, but perhaps you prefer something saltier and less expensive. However, "clean and nice" does not mean it is fit for the sea. If a boat is seaworthy, it can do more than one that is not. If the weather is foul, sometimes boats cannot get to good dive spots, yet they charge the same. Cover yourself by checking the operator's refund policy for bad weather and breakdowns.

Number of DiveCons or Divemasters Per Dive

Some operations cater to student and entry level divers, others to advanced. If you want supervision, look for a boat with enough professional divers to provide adequate coverage. If you do not, find one offering taxi service to and from the dive site. If a professional guide is not an included service, most boats will often provide one for an additional fee.

Length of Trip to Dive Site

For a spectacular dive spot, or if you love relaxing boat rides, a long trip might be worth the time. Of course, if you get seasick easily, a short ride would be preferable.

Galley

Live-Aboard Considerations

Because of the extended services of live-aboards, there are some special considerations for these vessels.

♦ *Overnight Accommodations:* Some provide bunks, while others feature beds. In private or semi-private cabins.

♦ *Meals:* Large ships have elaborate banquets, others serve a meal in the galley.

♦ *Showers:* Most boats expect you to take a "navy" shower to conserve water, while a few have plenty of it for you to enjoy.

♦ *Gear Storage:* Is there plenty of space for your equipment?

♦ *Safe Storage:* Is there a place for your valuables, such as your camera?

♦ *Photographic Darkroom:* It is becoming more common to offer E-6 processing for seagoing shutterbugs, and digital downloading.

Gear Storage on Boat

Safety Equipment Checklist

Because diving involves some calculated risks, the boat should have safety equipment available. The highest priority of any charter operation should be your safety. Personal boats should also have this equipment, because it is the captain's responsibility to handle any emergency. Below is a list of equipment and procedures considered the minimum by diving industry standards. It exceeds the requirements of the U.S. Coast Guard.

- ◆ Crew trained in CPR and First Aid
- ◆ First Aid Kit
- ◆ Oxygen
- ◆ Safe entry and exit points
- ◆ Fresh drinking water
- ◆ Easily available flotation device for diver in distress or passenger overboard
- ◆ Current lines, hang-off lines or safety stop bar
- ◆ Appropriate dive flags
- ◆ Diver orientation for boat safety, diving location, relevant conditions or hazards
- ◆ Professional diving supervisor, such as DiveCon or divemaster
- ◆ Written list of passengers aboard
- ◆ Shore communications
- ◆ Global Positioning System (GPS)
- ◆ Fire extinguishers
- ◆ Tool kit
- ◆ Extra dive equipment and spare parts
- ◆ License to operate

Shore Communications

For divers, hyperbaric chambers are a very important medical consideration, especially if you are in a remote area. Most popular dive spots now have chambers on island, or near by. Contact the Divers Alert Network in the U.S.A. at (919) 684-2948 for more information on diving accidents. On extended trips to remote locations, boats should have plans for handling medical emergencies. Personal boats should always have such a plan, including telephone and radio numbers, and the location of the nearest medical facility.

Dive Boat Checklist

Use this convenient checklist when selecting a dive boat. It condenses the critical items from the previous lists into criteria you can use to compare boats.

DIVE BOAT CHECKLIST

Name of Boat: _____

Date (s) of Trip: _____ to _____

Time of departure: _____ Time of Return: _____

Price of Trip: $ _____ Includes: _____
_____

• •

Safety equipment (y/n): _____ Safe entry/exit (y/n): _____

Proper license (y/n): _____

Captain's name: _____

Capacity: _____ Number of divers: _____

Galley (y/n): _____ Sun cover (y/n): _____

Dive Plan: _____

Dive destination(s): _____

Level of diving difficulty: _____

Number of tanks per dive: _____ Nitrox (y/n): _____

On-board compressor (y/n): _____ Air fill: $ _____

Comments: _____
_____
_____

Sources of information

There are many resources available to help you determine your needs and research information. These resources are available in most local bookstores and libraries, or through a few phone calls.

◆ Local SSI Authorized Dealer

◆ Scuba Schools International (SSI)

◆ Scuba Instructors

◆ Diving Magazines

◆ Travel Agents

◆ World Wide Web

◆ Friends

◆ Dive Clubs

◆ Travel Books and Magazines

◆ Tourist Bureaus

◆ Phone Books (where you are staying)

◆ Hotels, Motels, Bed and Breakfasts (where you are staying)

Selecting a dive boat is an important first step. To have the best time, it is important that you find one compatible with your needs. This requires you to make a few decisions about the kind of diving that you would like to do. Then, with a little research and some knowledge about the choices and options available, you should have enough information to make an appropriate selection. Remember, your local SSI Dealer and Instructor are there to help you when selecting a dive boat.

Section I Review Questions

1. The first step in diving from boats is _____ one.

2. Live-aboard boats feature _____, _____, _____, and an _____-_____ _____ _____.

3. Day boats take passengers to _____ _____ _____ within a distance easily covered in one half to one full day.

4. One of the most important steps in selecting a dive boat is _____ _____ _____.

5. To avoid dehydration on long, hot days, adequate _____ are essential.

6. Even if the boat looks right, you should also consider the diving it provides, how much it costs, and _____ _____ _____ _____.

7. The highest priority of any charter operation should be your _____.

8. On extended trips to remote locations, boats should have plans for handling _____ _____.

Preparing for Your Trip

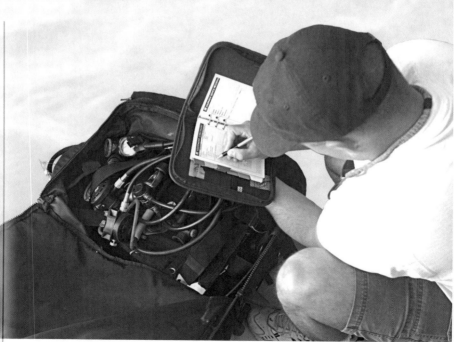

Now that you have learned about boats and selecting them, the next step is learning to prepare for trips. Miles from shore is not the place to discover you have forgotten equipment or are having problems with it. It is also not the place to realize you are in bad physical shape, that you are uncomfortable in the water, or that you are seasick and did not bring motion sickness medicine.

SSI
SCUBA SCHOOLS
INTERNATIONAL

Preparation
Diving from a boat requires total preparation, in all aspects.

DIVER
DIAMOND
SSI
KNOWLEDGE · SKILLS · EXPERIENCE · EQUIPMENT

Section 2 Objectives
After completing this section you will:

◆ Know how to pack your equipment,

◆ Know to get yourself ready through fitness and Scuba Skill Update,

◆ Know the different types of motion sickness medicines,

◆ Know how to prepare for any kind of boat dive or trip.

2

Getting Your Equipment Ready

Before you go on a dive boat, you should know that you have all the equipment you need and that it works and fits properly. You might consider taking the SSI Equipment Techniques specialty. This is a course designed for those interested in equipment maintenance and basic field repair. However, listed on the following page are steps for basic equipment preparation:

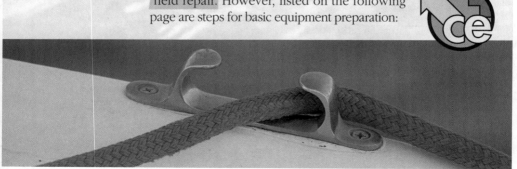

Use the Equipment Checklist

To ensure you have all your equipment, use the checklist included in your SSI Total DiveLog. It is quite embarrassing to arrive at the dive site miles from shore, only to discover you forgot to pack your mask.

Inspect Your Equipment for Problems

Replace damaged or worn straps, lubricate exposure system zippers, repair torn exposure systems, and make sure all of your equipment works well and is adjusted properly.

Inspect Your Equipment for Problems.

Equipment Service Program
The SSI Equipment Service Program

Your SSI Dealer may offer the SSI Equipment Service Program, a complete maintenance program designed to keep the components of your Total Diving System performing to the best of their potential. Below is an explanation of each of the services that make up the SSI Equipment Service Program.

Air Delivery System Protection

Regulators are totally disassembled and cleaned in a special cleaning solution. High-pressure and low-pressure seats are replaced along with all dynamic o-rings, exhaust valves, and high pressure filters. Performance tests are conducted to manufacturer warranty specifications.

Nitrox Air Delivery System Protection

This is the same as Air Delivery System Protection, but is performed on Nitrox equipment. A green Nitrox hose sleeve is used to mark your Nitrox Air Delivery System rather than a yellow hose sleeve.

Information System Protection

Submersible pressure gauges, depth gauges, pressure activated dive timers, and dive computers are checked for accuracy in a pressure vessel, and the indicated readings versus true readings are noted.

Buoyancy Control System Protection

Buoyancy compensators are inspected for buckle strap tension and bladder seam integrity. Inflator mechanisms are disassembled, cleaned and rebuilt, the inner bladder rinsed with B.C. conditioner and over-pressure release valves are cleaned and tested for proper operation, all to manufacturer warranty specifications.

Visual Inspection Protection (and Visual Plus®)

Annually, cylinders are inspected internally and externally for rust and corrosion to the standards of DOT and CGA. It is suggested that aluminum cylinders tested with Visual Plus to ensure the integrity and strength of the neck and threads.

Exposure System Protection

Services are available for exposure suits (wet and dry). Minor repairs are done in house and alterations are done with the original manufacturer.

When you have your equipment serviced or repaired, take along your SSI Total DiveLog so the technician can record the service. This will be valuable should you decide to upgrade your equipment someday.

Air Delivery Systems, Information Systems and Buoyancy Control Systems should be serviced at your local SSI Authorized Dealer at least once per year or as recommended by the manufacturer. These pieces of equipment are your life support, so make sure they work properly. After that, use them in a local pool to ensure they are adjusted correctly and work properly. To avoid problems, it is a good idea to have equipment serviced well in advance of trip departure dates.

Prepare a Spare Parts Kit

Nothing is more disappointing than arriving at a spectacular dive site, and having to sit out because of a minor equipment problem. That's why the spare parts kit is essential. Check with your local dive store for special recommendations, but be sure to include extra mask straps, fin straps, snorkel keepers, and cylinder o-rings in all popular sizes. Also, include mask defog.

Spare Parts Kit

Purchase New or Specialized Equipment

If a piece of equipment is old or worn out, it could be a good idea to replace it. If you have been thinking about completing your Total Diving System with a new air delivery system, now is the time to talk to your SSI Dealer. If you have just received training in a new area of the sport, such as photography or night diving, be sure to include equipment for that specialty. If you have all your basic scuba equipment, there are countless accessories that add new flavor to your experiences.

Mark All Equipment With Your Name

Use a waterproof marker and write your name or initials on every piece of equipment, including bags and dry boxes. On a crowded boat, it is likely that somebody will have the same equipment you have. By marking everything, you will avoid questions about ownership.

Mark Your Equipment

Packing Your Equipment

After your equipment is ready to go, the next step is packing it. For this you will need a large, sturdy dive bag. And for best results, the order in which you pack equipment is very important. Because boats are often crowded, you do not have much room to spread out, and your equipment can easily become mixed up with someone else's. When there is rough water, it can be a bouncy, rocking scramble to get into the water. For these reasons, some boats will ask you to stow all bags off the deck, or off the boat.

To facilitate dressing time and space, pack your equipment bag in a logical, efficient "reverse" order: on the top, pack equipment you will put on first; on the bottom, pack equipment you will put on last.

This way, you will take equipment from the bag as you need to put it on. The goal is to avoid digging through your bag to find the equipment. Here is a sample packing list:

Equipment Packed on the **BOTTOM**	Equipment Packed on the **TOP**
◆ Fins	◆ Exposure System
◆ Mask	◆ Booties
◆ Snorkel	◆ Air Delivery System
◆ Instrument box	◆ Buoyancy Control System
◆ Game bag	◆ Knife
◆ Gloves	

Note: *Weight belts with weights are not packed in the equipment bag, but are carried separately.*

Getting Yourself Ready

It is as important to prepare yourself for diving as it is your equipment. Being in good shape before a trip allows you to dive more often, and enjoy each dive more. Also, divers in good shape are better able to handle waves, currents, and their equipment, and to help other divers.

No matter what shape you are in, dive within the limits that you feel comfortable with.

2

Other sports and aerobic exercises are an excellent preparation for diving because they strengthen leg muscles and provide a cardiovascular workout. These would include:

♦ Running and Walking

♦ Swimming

♦ Swimming with Fins

♦ Bicycling (stationary or on the road)

♦ Aerobics

♦ Snorkeling

Of course, do not forget to eat healthy food. Eating right is as important as exercise. When diving, plan to eat light foods that are easily digested. Avoid spicy foods that produce stomach gas. Before a boat trip, make sure you get adequate sleep. And, as always, never dive after using drugs or alcohol.

Certification Card, SSI Total DiveLog, Dive Tables, Dive Computer

There are several important items you will not want to forget. First, without your certification card you will have trouble filling your cylinder, renting scuba equipment or joining a dive charter. Second, DiveLogs have become increasingly important. More boat operators are checking DiveLogs as an indication of diver activity and skill level. With the SSI Total DiveLog System, there is additional incentive to log dives. For example, to become a Specialty Diver you must log 12 dives and complete 2 specialty courses. To achieve Advanced Diver status, you must log 24 dives along with completing 4 total specialty courses, and when you add the Stress and Rescue course and log 50 total dives you can apply for the Master Diver card. After 100 dives, you are eligible for the prestigious Century Diver card.

Make sure you return to an SSI Dealer to receive recognition for your logged dives.

SSI LEVEL 2

SSI LEVEL 3

Master Diver

SSI LEVEL 4

SSI DIVE LEADER

SSI DIVE LEADER

Do not forget your dive tables for planning your bottom time. It is a good idea to practice a few sample dive profile problems, especially if it has been awhile since your last dive. You should review the tables even if you have a dive computer, in the unlikely event that it fails. If your computer does fail, make sure you wait 24 hours before switching to the tables. The profiles of dive computers and tables are not directly compatible, so you must first burn off all nitrogen in your body before switching. Before using your computer, review the unit's features and functions in the instruction booklet.

SSI Scuba Skills Update

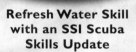

If you have not been diving for a year or more, you should consider an SSI Scuba Skills Update. This fun program is designed to refresh your basic diving skills and raise your personal comfort level, so you can maximize your diving time. It also includes many tips on planning a safe and enjoyable dive trip. It is available at your local SSI Dealer and is quick, easy, and inexpensive. It is a perfect way to brush up your diving skills, increase your comfort level and, most importantly, make you a better diver.

Refresh Water Skill with an SSI Scuba Skills Update

Motion Sickness Preventatives

One of the most unpleasant things that can happen to a diver on a boat is motion sickness. Not only is it a horrible feeling, but it is also recommended that you do not dive with motion sickness. Therefore, if you are likely to become seasick, you should prepare for the possibility by taking some preventative medicine with you.

Motion Sickness Medication

The strongest ones are pharmaceutical products, which should be taken only with the guidance of a physician. There are drug-free alternatives, as well as some good old fashioned home remedies that help if you are feeling nauseous. Which one you choose depends on your needs.

Scopolamine Patches®

Recently, many people who suffer motion sickness have started using Scopolamine patches. These small patches stick behind your ear, each patch lasting several days. You must obtain this medication from a physician. Tell the doctor you are a diver and describe the kind of diving you plan to do. Be sure to use them as prescribed, as they can have side affects.

Dramamine®

This is one of the original motion sickness medicines. Even though it is available over the counter, you still should consult a physician before diving while on this medication.

Acupressure For Wrist

This product is a terry cloth wristband with a plastic ball attached to it. By placing the plastic ball on a particular spot on the inside of your wrist, the ball can help stop motion sickness from occurring. The advantage of this product is that it is not a drug. The disadvantage is you must put the ball in the correct spot or it will not work.

Stomach Antacid and Hard Candy

This is a classic home remedy. First, you eat the stomach antacid which settles your stomach. Next, you have hard candy which induces some sugar into your system. The combination of ingredients acts quickly as a mild preventative. You can also use this remedy in combination with others, such as Dramamine®.

Pre-Trip Research

If you are going on a dive vacation, there are a variety of details related to boat diving that you can handle prior to leaving. Taking the initiative to research these details will enhance your vacation by maximizing your time and money, while avoiding problems. The more you know about where you are going, the more fun you are likely to have.

Best Season for Diving

Sometimes, the most popular travel times are not the best for diving. The busy season is the most expensive. Also, during the busy seasons, boats are more crowded and book up faster. The weather can be nicer during off-season, with calmer, warmer, clearer water.

Best, Most Famous Local Dive Sites

You should research the spectacular dives before you arrive. Knowing the history of wrecks and what local marine life to expect will enhance your experience and build excitement and anticipation. Also, if there is a particular dive you want to do, a little research could uncover a boat specializing in that dive.

Best Dive Stores

Many SSI dive stores operate boats, offer guide trips and vacations, and fun store clubs such as Club Aquarius Before you arrive, research who they are, their reputation, and services offered.

Best Charter Boat Operators

There are independent operators who are not affiliated with a dive store. They offer the same basic service as dive store boats, but do not sell or service equipment.

Special Equipment

The type of dive will determine any special equipment or accessories needed. If the water is cold you will want a hood and gloves, or maybe a dry suit. Perhaps you will need some filters for your camera, or an abalone iron and game bag. It's always a good idea to have warm clothing and extra towels also. If you do not have a spare parts kit, your SSI Dealer can help you put one together.

Special Paperwork

When going to a foreign country, do not forget your passport or to register your scuba and camera equipment with Customs to avoid paying unnecessary duty. If you plan to take game, you will need a fishing license. Research the seasons for the game you want, and cost of the license. As always, you will need your certification cards and SSI Total DiveLog for proof of certification and experience.

Helpful Boat Terminology

Boaters use a language all their own. To communicate effectively with crew members and knowledgeable passengers, you should learn a few simple terms, as shown below:

Aft – To the rear of the boat.

Bow – Forward end of a boat.

Below – Area beneath the deck.

Bridge – Where the boat is steered.

Deck – The floor of the boat.

Forward – To the front of the boat.

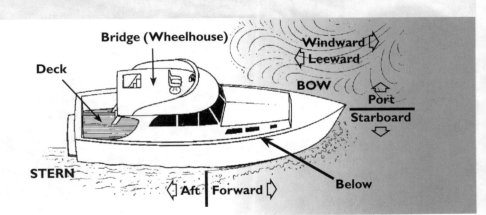

Galley – The boat's kitchen.

Head – The boat's toilet.

Leeward – Pronounced "loo'ard," away from the wind.

Port – Left, when facing the bow (forward). Here is a memory tip: "left" and "port" both have four letters.

Prop – The propeller that moves the boat.

Rudder – Underwater steering mechanism.

Starboard – Right, when facing the bow (forward).

Stern – Back end of the boat.

Wheel House – See "Bridge."

Windward – Into the wind.

Summary

Preparing for a boat dive or trip is your best way to maximize diving enjoyment. When you know your Total Diving System works properly and is well maintained, when you are confident in your diving skills, and when you are ready for problems, such as seasickness, you can relax and concentrate on having fun. Extra preparation, such as research and learning some basic boat language, will also enhance the experience and separate you from the others as a real boat diver.

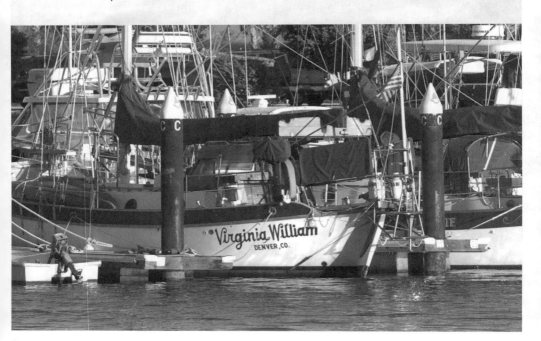

Section 2 Review Questions

1. Before you go on a boat, you should know that you have all the equipment you need and that it _____ and _____ properly.

2. Use a waterproof marker and write your _____ or _____ on every piece of equipment, including bags and dry boxes.

3. To facilitate dressing time and space, pack your equipment bag in a logical, efficient "_____" order.

4. Log books have become increasingly important. More boat operators are checking log books as an indication of _____ _____ and _____ _____.

5. If you are likely to become seasick, you should prepare for the possibility by taking some _____ medicine with you.

6. If you are going on a dive vacation, there are a variety of details related to boat diving that you can handle _____ _____ _____.

Traveling on Your Boat

After you arrive at the boat, there are several small tasks you should accomplish before it departs from the dock. Although it is fun to talk to the other passengers and savor the anticipation of upcoming dives, experienced boat divers first take a few minutes to make sure they have everything done. Then they kick back and relax, knowing there will not be any unpleasant surprises.

SSI
SCUBA SCHOOLS
INTERNATIONAL

Section 3 Objectives
After completing this section you will:

◆ Learn procedures for boarding a charter or personal boat,

◆ Learn about boat etiquette needed to be a thoughtful passenger,

◆ Learn proper dressing procedures.

3

Charter Boats

You should arrive at the dock about one half hour before departure time. By arriving early, you can get settled and familiarize yourself with the boat before others arrive. This is a good habit because boats operate on strict schedules, and you may not have the time you'd like to prepare for the trip if you arrive late.

Live-Aboards

Depending on the type of boat you are on, the crew may do everything for you, or you may do most of the work yourself. Typically, the crew will check you in and, in most cases, will assign a place for your equipment. After taking care of your equipment, find out about the overnight accommodations. The main types are private cabins or multiple bunks. If your boat has cabins, ask a crew member where your room is. If it has bunks, select one by putting your travel bag on it. Most bunks have different lengths and widths. If you tend to get seasick, try to find a bunk amidship (towards the center of the boat), because the bow and stern will pitch up and down much more than the middle.

Once you have a place to sleep, take some time to orient yourself to the boat.

◆ Find out where the head (toilet) is and ask how to use it, because they do work differently than toilets on shore.

◆ If there is a shower, find out when you can shower and whether "navy" shower rules apply. When taking a "navy" shower, you use water only to wet your skin and wash off soap.

◆ Locate the galley (kitchen) and find out about meal schedules and galley rules. For instance, sometimes you are allowed inside with a wet suit, sometimes you are not. Also find out about paying galley tabs.

◆ Inquire about diving procedures, and the location of fresh drinking water.

Find Out Where the Head is and Ask How to Use It

Day Boats

Since you are only going out for all or part of a day, the procedures are much simpler. After you stow your equipment bag, check the air pressure in your cylinder to ensure it is full. Next, set up your buoyancy compensator and air delivery system, and make sure everything works properly. Then, secure your cylinder. Check one last time that you have all necessary, but easily forgotten, equipment, such as mask and wet suit boots. As on live-aboards, find out where the head is and how to use it.

Check Air pressure in Your Cylinder to Ensure it is Full

Personal Boats

Because they are smaller and usually owned by friends, these boats do not have procedures so much as courtesies. However, the lack of formality does not mean a lack of etiquette. Follow the same basic steps as you would for a charter boat.

It is still good form to arrive well before you are scheduled to leave. You should still ask the captain where to stow your gear. To avoid arriving at the dive site with a half-full cylinder, check the cylinder pressure. If it is alright with the captain, set up your scuba unit and organize the remainder of your equipment. This saves time when you arrive at the dive site.

On a personal boat you should expect to help out with the crewing. For example, you may push the boat away from the dock, push the boat through the surf, load and unload the boat from its trailer, drop and pull up the anchor, and maybe even drive the boat, if you are qualified. As the guest, be ready to help out in any way, including hauling equipment aboard the boat and stowing it.

Notification

Prior to leaving, notify someone on shore that you will be on a boat and your expected time of return.

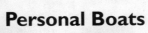
DIVER DIAMOND
SSI
KNOWLEDGE · SKILLS · EQUIPMENT · EXPERIENCE

Heads

Boat bathrooms, or heads, are different enough from those on shore to warrant a brief discussion. To avoid system blockages, the general rule of thumb is that anything you have eaten is acceptable to go in the head. In other words, non-organic items go into the trash. Disposal of toilet paper varies from boat to boat. Some do not want passengers to put toilet paper in the head, while others allow it.

On all boats, if you get seasick, do not use the head, use the leeward (away from the wind) rail, or stern of the boat.

Common Boat Etiquette

On any boat, chartered or personal, there are certain courtesies thoughtful passengers observe. Use of these courtesies should begin when you set foot on the boat. Most are common sense, but they are easy to forget when the fun begins. However, if you follow these simple guidelines, you will always be welcome back.

Captain or Owner is Boss

Whatever they say goes, because your safety and the boat are their responsibility. Use the entry and exit techniques they require, stow your equipment where they tell you, and obey the diving parameters they set before each dive. Especially in bad weather, do what the captain tells you.

Do not Drop Cylinders or Weights on Boat Deck

This could damage the deck, which would require expensive repairs. To prevent weights from slipping off the

belt, use weight clips or buckle the belt. Set heavy objects on the deck gently and do not leave cylinders standing unattended, especially when the boat is in rough water. Always use buddy assistance to don equipment and remove equipment.

Keep Your Equipment Organized

Before a dive, keep all your equipment organized in your bag, or in its designated storage spot. When you finish a dive, return all equipment to your bag as you take it off. This prevents clutter on the boat, confusion over ownership, and accidental equipment breakage, such as someone stepping on your mask.

Stay Clear of Crew's Work Area and Engine Room

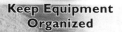
Keep Equipment Organized

Even though what they do is interesting, resist the temptation to watch the crew too closely, especially when they are handling a problem. Stay out of their way.

The engine room is strictly off-limits to passengers because of the potential machinery hazards.

Also, let the crew handle lowering and raising the anchor and mooring to buoys.

Obey All Boat Procedures

After you board, the captain will give a briefing on the boat's standard operating procedures. This will most likely include the layout of the boat, equipment storage, diving procedures, rest room facilities, safety regulations, seat assignments, dining routine, and emergency procedures. In the case of a personal boat, the owner will informally explain to you how they normally do things. As a passenger, these are your guidelines to having a fun trip, while still respecting the captain's or owner's property.

Make a Dive Plan with Your Buddy

While you are enjoying the ride, talk to your buddy about what kind of dive you want to make. You should also seek information from the captain, DiveCon or divemaster in charge. They will tell you the conditions to expect, depth, and what you are likely to see. With this information, you can create a dive plan before the boat anchors. Use your SSI Total DiveLog to start your pre-dive checklist.

Safety

If you are diving with a new buddy, make sure you both agree on all safety procedures.

KNOWLEDGE · SKILLS
DIVER DIAMOND
SS/
SCUBA SCHOOLS INTERNATIONAL
EQUIPMENT · EXPERIENCE

Practice Motion Sickness Prevention

Avoiding problems with motion sickness starts with prevention. Once you are seasick, it is too late; there is not much you can do about it. At that point, medication will not work; all you can do is try to get comfortable and off the boat as soon as possible.

When seasick, the decision to dive is with the diver. Some people believe the remedy to motion sickness is to dive. If you feel a little queasy, you might dive and not have a problem.

Make a Dive Plan with Your Buddy

If you are very seasick (vomiting) and choose to dive, keep in mind the consequences of that decision.

Some divers believe that sometimes the symptoms disappear once you are below the surface. But, the same surge and wave action that caused the boat to pitch and roll is present, to some extent, under the water. Therefore, that nauseous feeling can return. This can cause some very unpleasant and potentially dangerous possibilities, such as getting sick under water.

It is best to start motion sickness prevention before the boat leaves the dock. There are some simple habits that are effective, which are listed below. For best results, combine as many as you can, or all of them.

Take Your Medication Early

Do not wait until you are on the boat, that is too late. Take it up to two hours before the boat leaves the dock, to let it begin working. Follow the package instructions.

Do not Breathe Exhaust Fumes

Stay away from the back of the boat. This is where the exhaust is and where the least amount of fresh air is.

Stay in the Open Air

Breathing fresh air helps avoid nausea. To that end, do not go below deck if you can avoid it.

Stay Near the Center of the Boat

The least rocking motion is at the pivot point of the boat, both from side-to-side and from front-to-back, much like the center of a playground Teeter Totter.

The Steadiest Point of a Boat in the Center

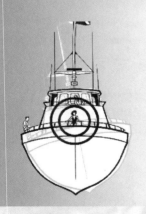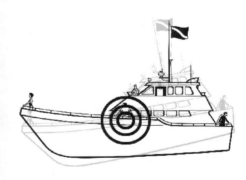

Eat Easily Digested Food

Avoid spicy or greasy dishes, as they tend to upset many people's stomachs. Sometimes soda crackers and clear, carbonated, caffeine-free beverages help settle your stomach.

Drink Plenty of Non-Alcoholic Liquids

Drink plenty of fresh water, especially if you are in the sun to keep the body hydrated. Alcohol and caffeinated drinks have the opposite effect and dehydrate the body. Staying hydrated not only helps combat motion sickness, it also lessens the body's susceptibility to Decompression Sickness.

Watch the Horizon

Concentrate on anticipating the boat's movements. This heightened sense of the boat's rhythm helps curb the seasickness.

Do not Read

Reading on a boat in rough water makes many people sick. If you are one of those people, pay attention to the boat, and save books and magazines until you get back to shore.

Drink Plenty of Water

Do not Get Overheated

Too much sun and wearing wet suits or dry suits can raise your core body temperature. Even a slight increase can make you nauseous, or lead to more serious problems such as heat exhaustion. If you feel too hot, remove excess thermal protection, get in the shade and drink fluids.

Try not to Think About Getting Sick

Relax, engage in conversation, and concentrate on the upcoming dive. By not focusing on getting sick, you may be able to prevent it, or at least lessen the severity. Also, although it might sound unfriendly, stay away from others who are seasick. Even though they do not mean to, they can adversely influence how you feel.

If you need to vomit because of seasickness, do not use the head (toilet). Instead, do it over the leeward (away from the wind) rail. Even though everyone will then know you are sick, you usually do not care at that point. Besides, there is no reason to be embarrassed. After all, no one is completely immune to *Mal De Mer*.

Getting Dressed

Try to avoid dressing too early, especially into your exposure suit, because you will probably be hot and uncomfortable by the time you enter the water.

Attend to the Boat

Having someone in the boat at all times who is capable of operating the boat and anchor system is a required practice. NEVER leave the boat unattended.

DIVER DIAMOND
SSI
KNOWLEDGE · SKILLS · EQUIPMENT · EXPERIENCE

Determine Timing for Dressing

Talk to the captain, DiveCon or divemaster to determine how long before the boat anchors and how long the pre-dive briefing will take, so you will know when to start dressing for the dive. Some boats will announce when to start, others will not. It is nice to get things organized so when it is time to dress, you can do it efficiently. This is the advantage of packing your equipment in reverse order.

Anchoring

On charter boats this is not a concern for you, because the crew takes care of it. However, on personal boats, where you are part of the crew, you need to know the fundamentals of good anchoring. Here are a few anchoring tips you should know.

All Passengers Checked Out

Everyone on the boat should be familiar with the anchoring system. Not simply what and where it is, but how to set it and, especially, to pull it up—competently—should the need arise. It is very unwise to assume that in an emergency situation only one person with these skills will be adequate.

Where to Set the Anchor

When the anchor is dropped, if you are over a coral reef, be extremely cautious about hooking it on the coral. Coral is not rock. It is a delicate, living creature. Try instead to set the anchor on a sandy bottom.

Anchor Line Tension

Leave enough line to absorb the shock of wave action, particularly in rough water. Otherwise, the anchor may be torn loose, causing the boat to drift away.

Do not Lay Equipment on the Anchor

That way you will not need to move it to drop the anchor, and avoid the risk of losing equipment.

Pre-dive Briefing

After anchoring, but before dressing, the captain will give a pre-dive briefing.

The main reasons for the briefing are to outline an overall dive plan and dive procedures.

For safety and enjoyment, each buddy team needs to fit their dive to the overall plan. And so that things run smoothly, everyone needs to know how the boat will manage the divers.

A Typical Briefing will Cover:

- ◆ Dressing Procedure
- ◆ Type of Dive or Underwater Activities at the Site
- ◆ General Direction of the Dives
- ◆ Maximum Depths and Bottom Time Limitations
- ◆ Minimum Air Supply Required Upon Ascent
- ◆ Expected Visibility and Currents
- ◆ Entering the Water and Reboarding the Boat
- ◆ Total Number of Dives
- ◆ Marine Life

Pre-Dive Briefing

Dressing

After the pre dive briefing, you will begin dressing. This is when the effort of packing in reverse order pays off, especially if the boat is crowded or on rough water. The biggest advantage is saving time. You will be able to dress more quickly and, because you have got a dive plan already, hit the water before anyone else. This is particularly important if the dive is an abalone or lobster hunt, a photography excursion, or located where a muddy bottom could be stirred by other divers. Getting dressed and into the water is not a race, however. The best pace is the one you feel most comfortable with.

For buddy teams, it is important to finish dressing at about the same time. That way, no one is waiting in a hot exposure suit.

Overheating is an uncomfortable situation. If you find yourself with a slower buddy, take your time.

Finish Dressing at the Same Time

Again, you are there to have fun, not to race. One way to improve the dressing process is to use buddy assistance. Buddies should help each other adjust straps, tuck in hoods, put on equipment, and make safety checks.

Remember to respect other people's space. Divers could be dressing elbow to elbow and do not have room to spread out equipment. Careful preparation and a well organized equipment bag make your experience more comfortable and fun.

In respecting other people, do not put on the scuba unit using the overhead method. This is especially dangerous in rough water, when maintaining balance is difficult. Even in calm water, you could seriously injure someone by striking them with the cylinder. Out of water, scuba units are heavy and awkward to handle.

Another typical safety rule is, do not walk with fins on. It is extremely easy to lose your balance, especially when the boat is rocking. On most boats, put on fins only before entering the water, and remove them before or as soon as you get out of the water.

Summary

Carefully anchoring the boat will make the difference between an excellent dive and a potential problem, either for you or the ecology. By establishing a good game plan, pre-dive briefings keep the group organized while preparing for contingencies. When dressing for the dive, safety and courtesy should be your main considerations.

Assist Your Buddy with Their Scuba Unit

Scuba Safety

For everyone's safety, including your own, put on the scuba unit using the safest, most appropriate method. This would include using buddy assistance or sitting on a bench to control the unit while you fasten and adjust it.

KNOWLEDGE · SKILLS
DIVER DIAMOND
SSI
SCUBA SCHOOLS INTERNATIONAL
EQUIPMENT · EXPERIENCE

Section 3 Review Questions

1. You should arrive at the dock about _____ _____ _____ before departure time.

2. On a personal boat you should expect to help out with the _____.

3. The general rule of thumb about what goes in the head is, anything you have _____ is acceptable.

4. It is best to start motion sickness prevention before the boat _____ _____ _____.

5. It is nice to get things organized, so when it is time to _____, you can do it _____.

6. After anchoring, but before dressing, the captain will give a _____-_____ _____.

3

7. Remember to respect other people's space. On a crowded boat, divers could be dressing _____ _____ _____.

Diving from Your Boat

4

After you have dressed, the next step is to enter the water. The transition from boat to water should be as easy and non-disorienting as possible, especially in cold, rough, or limited visibility water. In the pre-dive briefing, the captain should have outlined what to do, and properly trained boat divers know to obey these orders.

Section 4 Objectives
In this section you will learn:

◆ Proper entry and exit procedures,

◆ The basic diving guidelines to make your boat dive safer and more enjoyable,

◆ How to dive from any boat without difficulty.

The Boat Staff May Check You Out

Water Entry Procedures

In the pre-dive briefing, the captain, divemaster or DiveCon should have informed you of the entry procedures. If they did not, ask them before trying it, especially if it is your first time on the boat. On personal boats, the captain should still cover these procedures with the passengers. Although each boat has its own procedures, below is a typical list of steps:

Do not Enter Until "OK" is Given

The captain, DiveCon or divemaster manages the divers entering the water. Sometimes they use clipboards to record buddy teams and air pressure, and to check people out. This is so the crew has an accurate count of who is in the water. On a personal boat, it is usually less formal, simply let the captain know you are ready.

When it is Your Turn, Be Ready or Move Out of the Way

This is a courtesy, so you do not hold up the others. Make sure you have all equipment adjusted, air turned on, fins on, and mask in place or ready to rinse. If you are not ready, step aside and finish preparing.

Make Sure Your Air is on

Check your scuba cylinder valve to see if the air is turned on. You need to be able to breathe when you enter the water.

Have Air in Your BC

Partially inflate your BC so you will float as soon as you enter the water. Fully inflating is not necessary and may be less comfortable.

Have Your Fins on

One standard rule is divers are never allowed in the water without fins on. Without them, you have almost no control in the water. Then, even slight currents become dangerous because you can easily drift away, requiring someone to make a rescue. Most people sit on the platform side of the boat, or lean against their buddy to put them on. On platforms, be extremely cautious that you do not hit other divers as you sit down. Remember, don't walk on the boat deck with you fins on.

Make Sure Water is Clear of Other Divers

Before you step into the water, take a second to look for divers in the area. It is extremely bad form and dangerous to land on someone else. Not only can it cause lost equipment, such as knocking off masks, but cylinders can bump heads, causing serious injury.

Cover Your Mask and Second-Stage Regulator

To ensure your mask and second-stage regulator do not dislodge when you hit the water, hold the mask to your face and second-stage regulator in your mouth with your hand before stepping. Not only will this prevent lost equipment, but in cold water losing your mask is quite a shock to your face. A dislodged second-stage regulator in large swells could make breathing difficult.

Hold Weight System and Alternate Air Source

With your free hand, secure your weight system, alternate air source and instruments so that nothing is dangling as you leave the boat. Once in the water check your mask strap and weights to ensure they are properly positioned.

Have Accessories Handed to You

Do not get into the water carrying accessories. Spearguns can be dangerous, while cameras can be too delicate. Have these items handed to you after you are in the water and comfortable. Also, spearguns must be unloaded; never have a loaded speargun on the boat, or on the surface.

Wait For Your Buddy Before Descending

Buddy teams should always descend and ascend together. Do not wait for your buddy on the bottom, particularly in limited visibility water. Stay together so you can help each other with problems on descent, such as trouble clearing ears.

Types of Water Entries

Once you know the entry procedure, there are several standard water entries. The one you use will depend on the type of boat, the type of entry/exit points the boat has, and the water conditions.

Step In

This entry is most often used when the boat has a platform. This method is simple and works well in any water condition. To perform this entry, you stand on the platform, fins on, mask on, second-stage regulator in you mouth, and with air in your BC. Then you step off the platform, holding your mask and second-stage regulator in place with one hand and your weight system and alternate air source in the other.

Step-In Entry

When the water is rough, you must consider the boat's up-and-down movement when timing your step. Step off when the wave is at its lowest point. That way, if you misjudge the timing the wave will spring you up, which is better than having the boat drop from beneath you.

Controlled Seated Entry

This entry is best when the boat has a platform. It works well when the water is calm. With this entry you sit on the platform, which provides a solid foundation to put on your fins, rinse your mask, inflate your BC, and put the second-stage regulator in your mouth. Before you enter the water, make sure the area is clear of other divers. You want to avoid bumping anyone with your cylinder. When you know the area is clear, place both hands on the deck to one side of your body, shift your weight onto your hands, then spin slowly around toward your hands, gradually lowering yourself into the water. This allows a gentle, non-disorienting transition into the water.

Controlled Seated Entry

Jumping Entry

Sometimes boats do not have platforms, or you want to use a side exit point because the platform is crowded. In those cases, the distance from the exit point to the surface of the water might be several feet. The Jumping Entry works well because, just as you would not jump from a diving board with spread legs, you would not do so in scuba gear either. With your mask and fins on, some air in your BC, and second-stage regulator in your mouth, step away from the boat, holding your mask and second-stage regulator in place. Pull your legs together after you step from the boat. From the force of the fall, expect to go under water somewhat, but then to emerge because of the air in your BC.

Jumping Entry

Special Ladders

Some boats are now equipped with special ladders designed for use by divers wearing fins. They have wider footsteps and are angled about 45 degrees out from the boat, much like a staircase in a house. To enter, you simply put your fins on in the boat and walk down the ladder, facing the boat.

Back Roll

This entry is used from inflatable and other small personal boats when there is no diving platform and stepping into the water would be difficult, or would risk capsizing the craft. You must have all equipment adjusted and ready, mask and fins on, some air in your BC, and second-stage regulator in your mouth.

Backwards Roll

Hold your mask and regulator in place with one hand. To ensure nothing gets tangled, hold your instrument console and alternate air source with your other hand. Tuck your chin to your chest and roll backwards into the water. Once in the water, straighten up and let the BC float you. Pause for a moment, get oriented, and get out of the way so other divers can enter.

One consideration with the Backwards Roll is, while fun it can be somewhat disorienting, especially in cold water, because icy water can go down the back of your wet suit.

Putting the Unit on in the Water

Put on Scuba Unit in the Water

This entry relieves you of the need to enter the water with heavy equipment on. It works best in calm water with no current, and is often used from smaller boats. After inflating your BC, attach your scuba unit to a line and lower it into the water. Enter the water with your mask, fins, and snorkel in place. Whether you enter with a weight belt will depend on the captain's instructions and your comfort level. Once in the water, there are a variety of ways to put on the scuba unit. Which one you use depends on your training and personal preference. Once the unit is on, if you do not have your weight system in place, put it in place now. Pause for a moment, relax, and then descend when you and your buddy are ready.

Types of Boat Dives

There are many types of dives, some particular only to boats, others simply enhanced by them. The following list is typical of the common types of dives you will encounter. Most operators have special variations of these basic dives.

Diving Down the Anchor Line

Descend on an Anchor Line for Security

Basically, you follow the anchor line down to the bottom or to your desired depth, then proceed with your dive plan. The advantage is you have something secure to hold, which is useful when clearing ears, for keeping buddies together, or as a tether in currents and surges. A variation is the Drop Line (Descent/Ascent Line) which is a weighted rope attached to the boat and dropped straight down.

Drift Diving

In locations with substantial currents, drift diving is often the most practical way to dive. Divers simply float along effortlessly where the current takes them, with the boat following nearby. That way, the current is put to use rather than fighting it.

On drift dives, divers enter the water at the same time, descend together, and stay together throughout the dive. Staying together is a critical point. Otherwise, divers spread out, making group management nearly impossible.

There are a variety of drift dives. One style, called Float diving, gets its name because the dive leader holds onto a surface float that the boat follows. Another, called Anchor Line diving, involves divers holding onto a weighted line (not the boat's anchor line) attached to the boat. The boat drifts along with the engines off. Yet another style is called Live Boating, where the divers drift along while the boat follows their bubbles from a safe distance behind. Please note that, because of the currents, Drift Diving is considered an advanced activity, and should not be attempted by inexperienced divers, or divers uncomfortable in the water. Also, if the dive procedures are unclear, have the captain answer all questions to your satisfaction before entering the water.

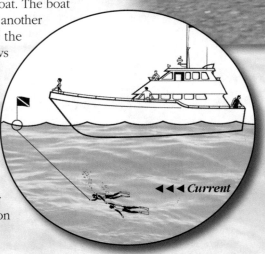

◀◀◀ *Current*

Float Diving

Wreck Diving

Many dive locations are famous for sunken ships, planes, or automobiles. Some areas deliberately submerge items to attract divers (artificial reefs). Wrecks can be fascinating, intriguing dive sites. Imagine seeing a sunken war ship or freighter; ships quite likely to be many times the size of the boat you came on. However, you must use common sense when diving on wrecks. Some wrecks are in very deep or cold water, have maze-like corridors in which you can easily become lost, and often accumulate fine silt which, when stirred up, can be disorienting. Therefore, diving them safely requires special training, and it can be risky if you do not know the potential, yet easily avoided hazards.

Wrecks can make Fascinating Dive Sites

If you are interested in wrecks, ask your local SSI professional dive store about the Wreck Diving specialty course. This fun, easy course will introduce you to wreck diving techniques, just as this course is preparing you for boat diving.

Game Taking

If you enjoy fish or shellfish, nothing tastes as good as seafood that you have caught yourself. Not only does it taste fresher, it has an additional element of satisfaction, much like eating vegetables harvested from a garden. Remember, be a responsible hunter by making sure you have the appropriate licenses, are within the correct season, and are observing game limit and size regulations. Some boats do not allow game taking, and in some countries, such as Australia, hunting is illegal.

4

Kelp Diving

For many, diving in kelp is one of life's pleasures. Kelp grows in large areas, forming a unique underwater forest. Prevalent on the Pacific Coast, these forests are home to fish, seals, and shellfish. Boats make many of the best kelp beds accessible to the average diver. If you have never dived in kelp, tell the captain. He or she will assist you. It is possible for cylinder valves, alternate air sources, and instrument consoles to snag on the kelp, mostly when swimming on the surface. However, you should not have a problem if you stay near your buddy; make sure you both have divers tools, and help each other when required.

Kelp is More Accessible from Boats

Night Diving

Diving is about exploring an accessible, foreign environment. Night diving takes that foreign environment one step beyond. You can dive a site during the day, and when you return at night, you can't believe you were in the same place. Certain creatures can only be seen at night. Today's powerful, long-lasting dive lights make seeing this exciting, surreal world possible. And, just as many of the best daytime dive spots are accessible only with boats, those same spots can be revisited at night with amazing, spectacular results. As with other forms of specialized diving, night diving requires additional training to ensure safe enjoyment. See your local SSI professional dive store about a fun and easy Night/Limited Visibility Diving specialty course.

Orientation and Navigation

It is extremely important to know where the boat is at all times during the dive. In tropical water with near-infinite visibility, this is usually not difficult. However, currents, kelp, and similar-looking reef formations can disorient you. In turbid water and on night dives, you often cannot see more than a few feet. And, on deeper dives, surfacing to determine your location is often impractical. There are a variety of problems, such as other boats, decompression

Use a Compass to Orient Yourself to the Boat

considerations, and drifting with the current. Therefore, before the dive starts you should orient yourself to the anchor, a unique reef formation, or other major underwater landmark. Depth, direction, and time are the primary components of this orientation, and the depth gauge, compass, and timer are the instruments used. To learn more, ask about the Navigation specialty course at your nearby SSI professional dive store.

Currents

In the pre-dive briefing, the captain should alert you about the direction and strength of the currents. On personal boats, you must determine it yourself. To do this, watch the direction the boat shifts before or while it is being anchored. Another way is to watch the direction the kelp drifts.

Once you determine its direction, the rule is to swim *into* the current at the start of the dive, and ride the current back to the boat at the end of the dive.

Swimming into the current can be physically difficult, so you want to do it before you are tired—at the start of the dive. However, be aware that there may be a current at depth, but not at the surface. Also, currents can go different directions at different depths. For more information about recognizing and dealing with currents, check into a Waves, Tides and Currents specialty course.

Air Management

One fundamental rule of diving is to monitor your air supply, and it is even more important when diving from a boat. In the pre-dive briefing, the captain will outline the boat's policy on minimum cylinder air pressure when returning. Make sure you include enough air for a 3-5 minute, 15 foot (5 metre) safety stop. A typical policy is to locate the boat with approximately 1000 PSI (70 bars), and be back aboard with not less than 500 PSI (35 bars). If at 1000 PSI (70 bars) you do not know where the boat is, surface and locate it. Another common rule is to swim away from the boat as far as 1/3 of your air supply will take you, so you have 1/3 to swim back, and 1/3 for reserve.

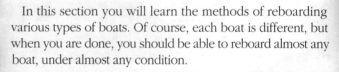

The 1/3 cylinder, or 500 PSI (35 bars), reserve is for use in case of emergencies.

The deeper the dive, the greater the reserve needed. The important thing is to use good diving habits: monitor your air constantly and never push your air supply to the limit.

Recall Systems

These are underwater speakers that signal divers to return to the boat in case of a diver emergency or deteriorating weather. They are used mainly on charter operations. If you hear the recall signal, surface immediately and look to the boat for instructions.

In this section you will learn the methods of reboarding various types of boats. Of course, each boat is different, but when you are done, you should be able to reboard almost any boat, under almost any condition.

Ways to Return to the Boat

Usually, there are one or more lines in the water to help divers ascend and get back to the boat. They are also used to help divers maintain a constant depth during safety stops prior to surfacing, especially when the current is strong. In a current,

divers making a safety stop can be pushed quite a distance from the boat if they do not have a line to hang onto. Since it has been well documented that a 15 foot (5 metres) safety stop greatly decreases nitrogen and has been recommended on any dive deeper than 30 feet (10 metres), the lines become quite valuable to divers.

Anchor Line

The anchor line is a good place to make a safety stop at the end of your dive or to hang onto during ascents.

A Drop Bar for Decompression Stops

Drop Lines

Drop lines, also called Ascent/ Descent lines, are weighted lines attached to the boat and dropped straight down into the water. Like anchor lines, they are useful during safety stops or to hang onto during ascent.

Drop Bars

These are bars hanging approximately 15 feet (5 metres) below the surface, used mostly for group safety stops. The advantage of a bar over a line is that many divers can make the safety stop simultaneously, where a line can accommodate only a few at a particular depth.

Current Lines

These lines extend from the stern of the boat, floating on the surface in the direction of the current. At the end of a dive in a strong current, it is possible to surface behind the boat. Divers grab the line and pull themselves to the boat using their arms.

Boat Re-Entry Procedures

On charter boats, re-entry procedures should have been covered in the pre-dive briefing. On personal boats, the captain should have discussed the procedures with the passengers. Although every boat has its own procedure, typical steps are listed below.

Current Line

Wait Your Turn

Most times, the divers will surface at different times, so there should not be a huge group at the platform. However, on drift dives, the entire group descends and ascends together. In any case, it is best to be patient and wait your turn to get back on the boat. Like any situation when everyone is trying to do something at once, it can become unsafe.

Stay Clear of Platforms

Especially in rough water, the boat rocks up and down. A diver under the platform or boat bottom could be struck on the head. This could cause a serious injury. Stay away from the boat until it is your turn to come aboard.

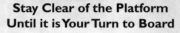

Stay Clear of the Platform Until it is Your Turn to Board

Stay Clear of Other Divers

Due to waves or loss of balance, a diver on a ladder or platform may slip and fall back into the water. If that happens, make sure you are not below the diver on the ladder. This is a dangerous situation because you could be struck by their cylinder.

Keep Mask on and Second-Stage Regulator in Your Mouth

Again, due to waves or loss of balance, you could fall back into the water. If this happens, at least you will be able to breathe and see. You should have air in your BC so you will float.

Wait
Until the diver in front of you has gotten completely aboard the boat before moving to climb up.

Hand Accessories to Crew

Do not attempt to board the boat while holding extra equipment. Either hand it to a crew member, place it far enough back on the platform so it will not fall back in, or place it in the boat. Extra equipment impedes your ability to re-enter the boat safely.

Types of Boat Re-Entries

Larger boats tend to have two basic methods for re-entering the boat: platforms and ladders. Some smaller boats, including rubber boats, have neither.

Boats With Platforms

These are areas behind the boat submerged a few inches below the water. They make a stable transition from water to boat. Usually they fold up when the boat is moving, and are lowered into the water for diving. Some have ladders, some do not. To re-enter a boat with a platform you would first place unloaded spearguns and cameras on the platform. Next, remove your weight system and place it on the platform. Leave fins and mask on and leave the second-stage regulator in your mouth. Leave your fins on because, once on the platform, it is possible to fall back into the water. Without fins, a diver has difficulty swimming effectively, which is hazardous in a current. After removing your weight system, climb onto the platform, staying on your hands and knees for better balance, in case of swells. Once you are stable on the platform, remove your fins and climb into the boat.

Stay on Your Knees for Better Balance

Boats With Ladders

The ladders sometimes go directly into the boat or onto a smaller platform area at the back of the boat. Ladders going into the boat are trickier because you must lift yourself out of the water and climb into the boat. Ladders going onto a small platform are considerably easier because you only have to climb to the platform, then into the boat. Either way,

to perform a ladder re-entry you must wait until the previous diver is safely in the boat. Next, place your accessories on the platform or in the boat, or hand them to a crew member. Leave your mask on and the second-stage regulator in your mouth. After you have a firm grip on the ladder, remove your fins. Take the fins off because it is difficult to place your feet on the ladder steps with them on. When they are off, either hand your fins to a crew member, put them on the platform so they will not fall back in, place them in the boat, or put your arm through the fin straps. Climb up the ladder, being careful not to slip. The weight of the equipment will become noticeable after a step or two up the ladder.

If Boat Has Neither

Some smaller boats do not have platforms or ladders. In that case, you will have to remove your heavy equipment to re-enter the boat. With it on, you are too heavy to pull yourself in. The captain will explain the procedure, but you will probably place accessories in the boat or hand them to someone in the boat. Next, remove your weight system by either handing it to someone in the boat or to your buddy, or by putting it in the boat. Then, making sure you have enough air in your BC so it will float, remove your scuba unit and either tie it to a line, or hand it to your buddy or to someone in the boat. With your mask and fins still on, grab the top of the boat with both hands. Using a powerful kick, thrust yourself out of the water and pull yourself into the boat.

Take Off Your Fins Before Climbing the Ladder

Use a Powerful Kick to Thrust Yourself out of the Water

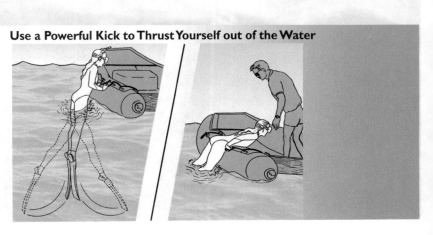

What to Do in Rough Water

Be Aware

After the dive, you may be tired. Therefore, getting back into the boat safely should be your most important consideration. Be aware of the water conditions, the other divers, and the boat. Also, make sure you can always breathe and float while climbing into the boat.

In rough water, the boat will rock up and down with the waves. You need to time your entry on the platform or ladder when the boat is at the low point. This is because the ladder or platform will drop unpredictably when at the high point, which could cause injury. However, at the low point, a sudden rise is manageable. People can handle being pulled up better than being dropped down.

What to Do if You Lose the Boat

If you pay attention to navigation and the effects of the current, this should never happen to you. However, if you do lose track of the boat, or the current sets you adrift, follow the procedures below:

♦ **Remain calm—you will be missed.**

♦ **Inflate your BC—drop your weights if necessary.**

♦ **Stay close to your buddy.**

♦ **Remain in the general area, if possible, unless you are very close to land.**

♦ **Use your whistle and/or other signaling device.**

The most important thing is to stay calm. Your priorities should be to stay afloat, conserve your energy, stay as warm as possible, and make it easy to rescue you. On personal boats, the time it takes to rescue you will depend on whether you told someone where you were going and when you would be back.

Signaling Device

Section 4 Review Questions

1. The transition from boat to water should be as _____ and _____-_____ as possible.

2. One standard rule is, divers are never allowed in the water without _____ on.

3. When the water is rough, you must consider the boat's _____ _____ _____ movement when timing your step.

4. In locations with substantial currents, _____ _____ is often the most practical way to dive.

5. Once you determine its direction, the rule is to swim _____ the current at the start of the dive, and ride the current _____ to the boat at the end of the dive.

6. If you hear the _____ _____, surface immediately and look to the boat for instructions.

7. Larger boats tend to have two basic methods for re-entering the boat: _____ and _____.

4

Finishing Your Boat Trip

5

SCUBA SCHOOLS INTERNATIONAL

Once you are back on the boat, it is tempting to start sharing stories with the other divers right away. However, the same situation that occurred when everyone was dressing will happen again, once the equipment comes off.

Therefore, experienced boat divers know it is easier and less stressful to take care of their equipment before they start socializing.

Section 5 Objectives
After completing this section you will:

♦ Learn everything you need to do after the dive is over. This includes:

• stowing equipment,

• logging the dive,

♦ Learn what to do on live-aboards, multi-cylinder dives, and day charters,

♦ Know how to end the dive like a real boat diver.

Check in With Captain/DiveCon

As soon as you are aboard, there should be someone ready to record that you are back from the dive. If no one is around, remove your equipment, find the person responsible, and let them know you and your buddy are aboard. The same is true on personal boats; tell the captain you are back. This will prevent a situation where the captain is concerned that you are not back from the dive, when in fact you are sunning on the deck.

Check Back in with the DiveCon or Captain

Stow Equipment

As soon as you are checked in and have removed your equipment, make certain you take proper care of it. If the boat has dunking containers or fresh water rinsing stations, rinse off your equipment. This removes salt if you have been diving in the ocean. Place mask, fins, and other small pieces of equipment in your bag or storage space immediately. This prevents any mix-up of equipment. If you are going to dive later in the day, repack in reverse order. The important thing is to keep your gear together and to make sure you have all equipment you came with, including small items such as defog.

Remember,

with the SSI Total DiveLog System, the dives count towards advanced certification. But more importantly, years later, your DiveLog will be a valuable scrapbook of diving adventures, sparking wonderful memories of past dives and buddies.

Log the Dive

As soon as you take care of your equipment, take care of your paperwork. Find your buddy and, together, log the dive. Record important information from your computer accurately, such as depth and time, because it will influence your repetitive dive profile. Also, take the time to record significant details such as big fish you saw, beautiful reef formations, or an impressive wreck. With the SSI Total DiveLog System it only takes a couple of minutes and is easy to do.

Log Your Dives

Multi-Cylinder Dive or Live-Aboard

If you are going to dive later in the day, you should take care of these items:

♦ **Set up your cylinder for the next dive**

♦ **Eat something light**

♦ **Drink plenty of decaffeinated, non-alcoholic liquids**

♦ **Plan your repetitive dive**

Diving is a calorie-consuming sport, and the dry compressed air tends to dehydrate you. To avoid problems, make sure you take care of your body before the next dive.

Renew your Energy Between Dives

Drink as much water as possible throughout the day.

Also, even if you are using a dive computer, it is extremely important to plan your surface interval, and repetitive depth and time.

One-Cylinder Dive or Day Charter

If you are only making one dive for the day and are heading back to shore, you should take care of these items after arriving at the dock:

◆ **Settle galley tab (if applicable)**

◆ **Tip crew (see below)**

◆ **Wash exposure suit and other equipment thoroughly with clean, fresh water**

◆ **Hang exposure suit and other equipment to dry, out of direct sunlight**

Personal Boats

Be prepared to help out in any way with the crewing. Possible jobs might include tending lines, loading the boat onto its trailer, beaching a rubber boat, or washing the bottom. Always offer to help unload cylinders and equipment.

5

Tipping

Showing your appreciation for good service should not stop in restaurants and bars. Diving professionals deserve recognition as well, for their hard work. Usually the divemaster or DiveCon gets the tip. The proper amount of the tip depends on the situation:

◆ **On Longer Trips.** 15% of the package price is common. Or, you can pay a flat rate per day.

♦ **On Day Trips.** Flat $5 - $15.

♦ **On Some Islands.** Hard to find personal items. These presents are highly appreciated because of their novelty and rareness. They are seen as status items that no amount of money can buy. For example, a new snorkel or dive knife not available locally would cause great excitement. Of course, this would be appreciated more in remote locations with less access to equipment.

Summary

The feeling after a day of boat diving is quite possibly as good as it gets. It is a thoroughly satisfying feeling of being both tired and fulfilled. Once you have docked or loaded a boat at sunset, unloaded your equipment, and then shared stories afterward with your fellow divers, you will be hooked. After that, you will realize what it means to be a boat diver, and boats will become more than just transportation. You will see that, somehow, the special sort of camaraderie fostered by diving is enhanced even more when boats are involved. Once you feel it, boat diving will forevermore have special meaning. Hopefully this Boat Diving Specialty course sparks a lifetime of memorable, rewarding experiences that diving can provide.

Section 5 Review Questions

1. As soon as you are aboard, there should be someone ready to record that you are _____ _____ _____ _____.

2. Place mask, fins, and other small pieces of equipment in your _____ or _____ _____ immediately. This prevents any mix-up of equipment.

3. Find your buddy and, together, _____ _____ _____.

4. The proper amount of _____ depends on the situation.

SCUBA SCHOOLS
INTERNATIONAL

Appendix

Index

Student Answer Sheet Directions

- Transfer your study guide answers to the following five Answer Sheet pages.

- Remember to write your name and the date on each page.

- Sign each page after you have reviewed each incorrect answer with your instructor.

- Your instructor will collect these pages during your Deep Diving course.

STUDENT ANSWER SHEET

SCUBA SCHOOLS
INTERNATIONAL

STUDENT NAME   PART #   DATE

Reviewed and Corrected by Student and Instructor:

STUDENT SIGNATURE   INSTRUCTOR SIGNATURE

1. _____
2. _____
3. _____
4. _____
5. _____
6. _____
7. _____
8. _____
9. _____
10. _____
11. _____
12. _____
13. _____
14. _____
15. _____
16. _____
17. _____
18. _____
19. _____
20. _____

STUDENT ANSWER SHEET

STUDENT NAME   PART #   DATE

Reviewed and Corrected by Student and Instructor:

STUDENT SIGNATURE   INSTRUCTOR SIGNATURE

1. _____
2. _____
3. _____
4. _____
5. _____
6. _____
7. _____
8. _____
9. _____
10. _____
11. _____
12. _____
13. _____
14. _____
15. _____
16. _____
17. _____
18. _____
19. _____
20. _____

STUDENT ANSWER SHEET

SCUBA SCHOOLS
INTERNATIONAL

STUDENT NAME   PART #   DATE

Reviewed and Corrected by Student and Instructor:

STUDENT SIGNATURE   INSTRUCTOR SIGNATURE

1. _____
2. _____
3. _____
4. _____
5. _____
6. _____
7. _____
8. _____
9. _____
10. _____
11. _____
12. _____
13. _____
14. _____
15. _____
16. _____
17. _____
18. _____
19. _____
20. _____

STUDENT ANSWER SHEET

STUDENT NAME   PART #   DATE

Reviewed and Corrected by Student and Instructor:

STUDENT SIGNATURE   INSTRUCTOR SIGNATURE

1. _____
2. _____
3. _____
4. _____
5. _____
6. _____
7. _____
8. _____
9. _____
10. _____
11. _____
12. _____
13. _____
14. _____
15. _____
16. _____
17. _____
18. _____
19. _____
20. _____

STUDENT ANSWER SHEET

SCUBA SCHOOLS
INTERNATIONAL

STUDENT NAME   PART #   DATE

Reviewed and Corrected by Student and Instructor:

STUDENT SIGNATURE   INSTRUCTOR SIGNATURE

1. _____
2. _____
3. _____
4. _____
5. _____
6. _____
7. _____
8. _____
9. _____
10. _____
11. _____
12. _____
13. _____
14. _____
15. _____
16. _____
17. _____
18. _____
19. _____
20. _____